"Tall Tales" and Other Truths

An exhibition which includes work by Aliza Augustine, a Holocaust survivor's daughter who documents other Holocaust survivor daughters telling their parents stories, Francis Crisafio, an artist of Italian descent whose photographs of his father's barbershop speak of 80 years of culture and community, Michael Pribich, an artist of Mexican descent who speaks of his family and history of the area they came from, Adrienne Wheeler, whose family history spans 200 years in Newark, NJ who creates works which document ancestry and family history, Noelle Lorraine Williams, a Newark artist showing works from her "Monumental Spirit: Re-imagined Sites of 19th Century" which depict Newark's Black Abolitionist Historical Monuments recontextualized, and Willie Cole, a critically acclaimed NJ-based artist transforms steam irons, ironing boards, hair-dryers, and high-heeled shoes into powerful sculptures, installations, and works on paper.

DRAWING ROOMS • 926 NEWARK AVE • JERSEY CITY, NJ

VICTORY HALL PRESS

Drawing Rooms is a nonprofit art space operated by Victory Hall Inc., a 501(c)(3) nonprofit organization producing exhibitions, programs and public art projects in the NJ/NY area since 2001:

Executive Director: James Pustorino
Exhibitions Director / Curator: Anne Trauben
Contact: victoryhall1@msn.com
Visit: www.drawingrooms.org

"Tall Tales" and Other Truths

"Tall Tales" and Other Truths
2/16/23 - 4/22/23

Curator's Statement

This show is personal.

Visual artists speak through images, sounds and experiences which often tell stories, either directly or indirectly. Stories, or narratives, aka Narrative Art, include made-up stories based in fantasy or imagined realities, stories composed of disparate elements used to create an inferred narrative, or stories which speak truth, either personally for the artist, or for people and/or issues the artist feels strongly resonates with them. Some artists choose to make this truth-work because they feel compelled to understand the issue better for themselves. Others do so to bring an issue out of the darkness and into the light, in the hope of helping to create awareness.

The artists in this show tell stories which personally relate to their ancestry, culture and community. These stories may involve secrets long kept unknown or unseen by others, whether nefarious or not, which people of one culture may not know about another person's culture, or people may not want others to know. The artists are engaging within the realm of Identity Art.

The stories of identity these artists tell run the gamut from exploration of one's cultural identity, to family joy, to painful and/or disturbing truths, to say the least, which, at one point or another, we all may have been told, or have heard others say are exaggerated or not based in truth. This, compounded by the fact that we are bombarded with "false news" and "alternative realities", makes the show timely and important. All the stories these artists are telling us are true, and their stories need to be shared and heard.

Presenting these stories brings truth to light, but can be complicated because they may create a sense of vulnerability for both the artist and the viewer.

Noelle Lorraine Williams works show us changes Newark, NJ has undergone, and a history of African Americans and African American culture we may know little about– a history which is downplayed– one in which much may be new to us, that we feel uncomfortable knowing about and may have even been told could not be true.

Willie Cole creates works which celebrate African art and culture and confronts viewers with the painful history of slavery in America.

Adrienne Wheeler's family spans more than 200 years and six successive generations in Newark, NJ. Her works document her ancestry and tell the viewer, "We've been here and continue to be here; our family history is important to know about".

Aliza Augustine, the daughter of a Holocaust survivor, helps dispel the disbelief of the difficult truths of the Holocaust by showing us Theresienstadt Concentration Camp. Her interviews with daughters of survivors are presented via photomontage in a dream-like way which makes their recalled stories both approachable and horrific at the same time.

Michael Pribich's grandparents crossed the border from Mexico, became US citizens and raised a family of nine children, one of which is his mother. The shawls in his *Seven Beauties* are life-size and stand-in physically for the bodies of seven sisters, while the rope represents the border immigrants cross with hope of succeeding in their new country. His *Black Support* imagery refers to the African slave ships brought to Mexico in 1521, and issues around Mexican labor history.

Francis Crisafio spent the last 10 years of his Italian American immigrant father's life documenting the haircut and shave barbershop he opened in 1929, during the Great Depression, and ran for 80 years in the Lawrenceville neighborhood of Pittsburgh, PA. In his *Together* series, Francis presents snapshots from the barbershop which include text identifying how long the customer had been loyal to Tony, his service, and the barber shop. Tony's customers were from all reaches of the community, including multi-generational families whose demographics spanned age, class, gender and ethnicity. Tony's barber shop was an important and stable fixture in the fabric of the community, providing a space for people of all walks of life to interact and connect, share stories and secrets from one customer to another, and between the customer and his/her favorite barber, Tony. Over time, Francis came to see his father in a new way and understand that Tony's loyal customers were his family too, as "they helped put food on our table."

Anne Trauben
2/24/23

ADRIENNE WHEELER
Newark, NJ

Adrienne Wheeler is a visual artist, independent curator and arts educator living and working in Newark, NJ. Her family history spans 200 years in Newark, NJ. Adrienne's visual arts practice blurs the lines between spirituality, ancestry, oral history, and social engagement. She has exhibited and curated locally and internationally in Cuba, Senegal and Australia. The work she's created individually and collaboratively is in public and private collections in the Newark Public Library, The Metropolitan Museum of Art and the Whitney Museum of American Art.

During the Great Migration and second Great Migration (1910-1970), African-Americans in search of better jobs, educational opportunities, and decent housing fled the Jim Crow South with many settling in Newark, New Jersey. Wheeler's mother and grandmother left Bainbridge, Georgia and arrived in Newark, New Jersey in 1937, when her mother was nine years old.

White Dress Narratives (opposite page)
This piece is a gathering of nine dresses representing six successive generations of women from Wheeler's maternal line. The dress was inspired by a white dress her mother made for her own 1942 graduation from Morton Street Elementary School, Newark, New Jersey. The stitched patterns on each dress illustrates each woman's story. The women are Adeline, Willie Kate, Ruby, Elizabeth, Adrienne Elaine, Lydia Blanche, Leah Carroll-Avis, Nadirah Elizabeth, and Mariyam Sahar. The information contained within each dress is drawn from multiple sources: census documents, marriage, birth and death records, historical data, historical fiction, memory, and interviews.

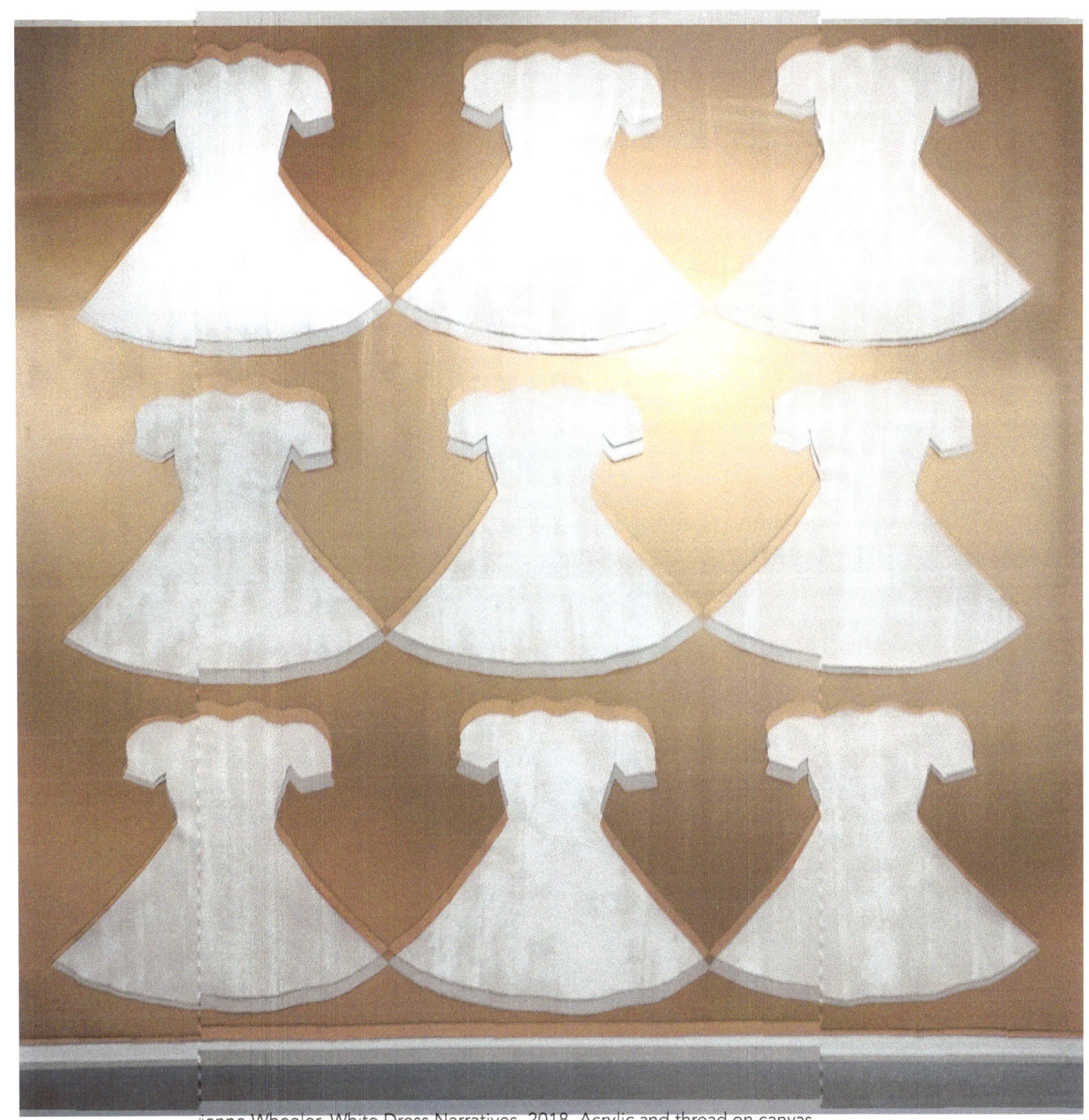

Adrienne Wheeler, White Dress Narratives, 2018, Acrylic and thread on canvas, 11' x 12'

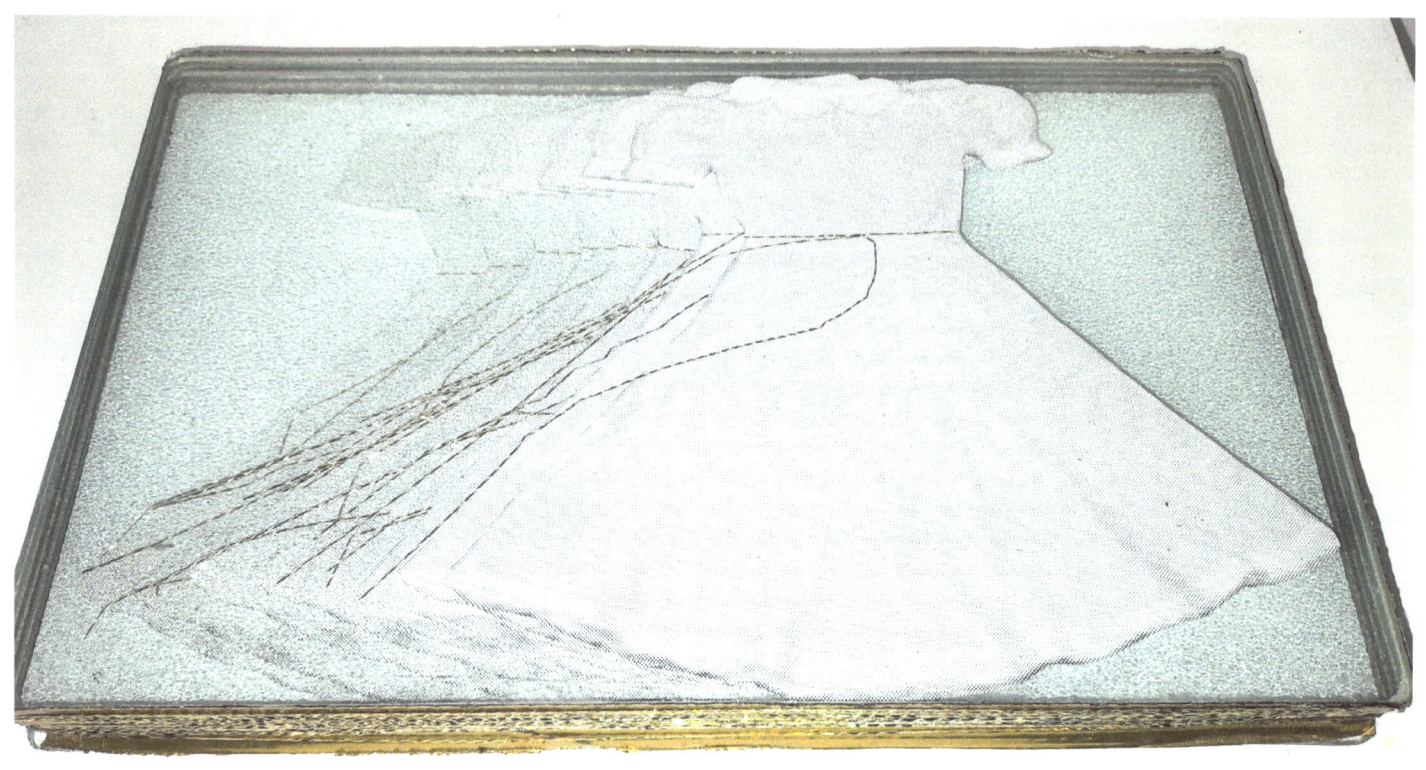

Adrienne Wheeler, Elizabeth, 2015, Mixed media sculpture, glass, paper, gold duct tape and thread. 5" x 8"

Adrienne Wheeler was Artist-in-Residence in 2015 for Provisions, the tenth iteration of the Glass-Book Project, with founder Nick Kline at Rutgers University.

Ingress:Egress (opposite page)
This piece is a silkscreened glass sculpture that is one component of The Wheeler Project: These Sacred Texts, an ongoing series that chronicles Adrienne's investigations of her paternal lineage. The Wheeler family history in the city of Newark, NJ is one that spans over two hundred years and seven successive generations of a family who have called Newark home. Included in the list of materials collected for this project are an 1830 enumeration record of free inhabitants, census documents, military records, and a wedding certificate. In the absence of family photographs, Wheeler has chosen to collect and assemble these documents in a glass sculpture, prints on paper and a multi-channel video installation. At its core, the work examines how histories are maintained and erased, and who or what determines their fate. "The work is personal and essential, it says we were here."

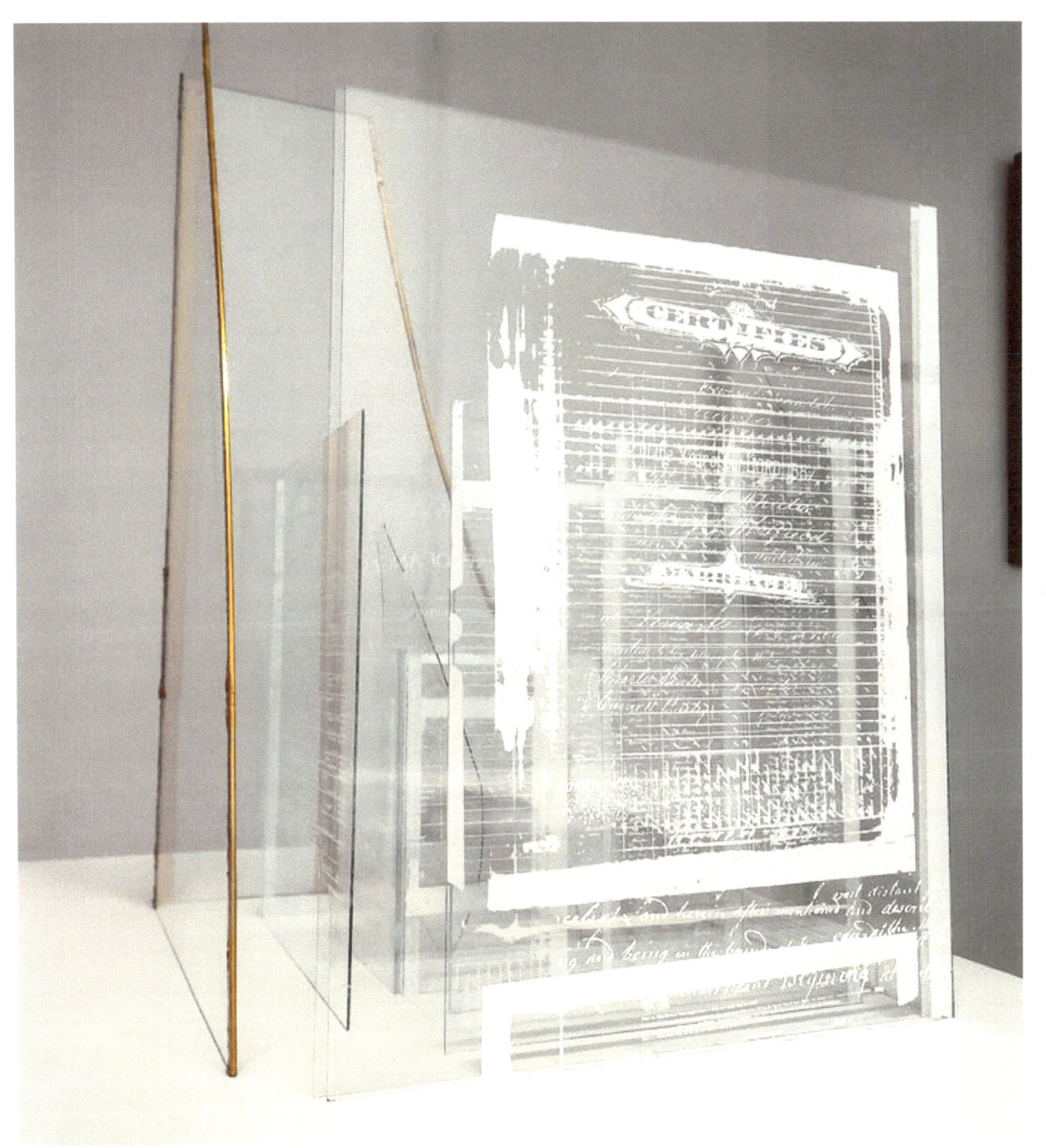

Adrienne Wheeler, Ingress:Egress, 2019 to present, Silkscreen on glass, 20" x 12" x 12"

ALIZA AUGUSTINE
North Bergen, NJ

Aliza Augustine is a narrative oil painter turned fine art photographer. Her diverse and opinionated family inspires her work, which is usually political. Mostly immigrants, Aliza's family comes from Poland, France, England, Israel, Vietnam, Canada, Germany, Columbia and Italy and are a mix of Jews, Buddhists, Atheists and Catholics. They are Ashkenazi, White, African-American, Latino and Asian. Aliza's family is the proud melting pot.

Some venues Aliza's work has been shown in include the Jersey City Museum, Westbeth Gallery, the College of St. Elizabeth, as part of Rutger's Feminist Art Project, and the Whitney Biennial. Internationally, her work has been shown in Berlin, Lisbon and Barcelona.

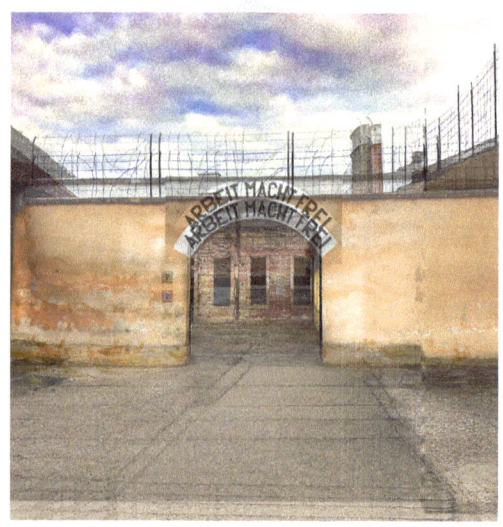

Aliza Augustine,
Arbeit Macht Frei,
Photo, 12" x 12", 2023

Terezín/Theresienstadt (above)
These photos were taken on an iPhone during the artist's visit to Terezín, a Concentration Camp in the middle of a town where today people have returned to live.

The purpose of the Theresienstadt ghetto was threefold: (i) as a holding point to concentrate most of the Jews from Bohemia and Moravia, as well as certain categories of Jews from Germany and western Europe — prominent individuals — those of achievement in the arts or in cultural life, as well as the aged and infirm; (ii) as a transit camp from which to transfer Jews to the extermination camps and (iii) to conceal the extermination of European Jews from the rest of the world by presenting Theresienstadt as a "model Jewish settlement".

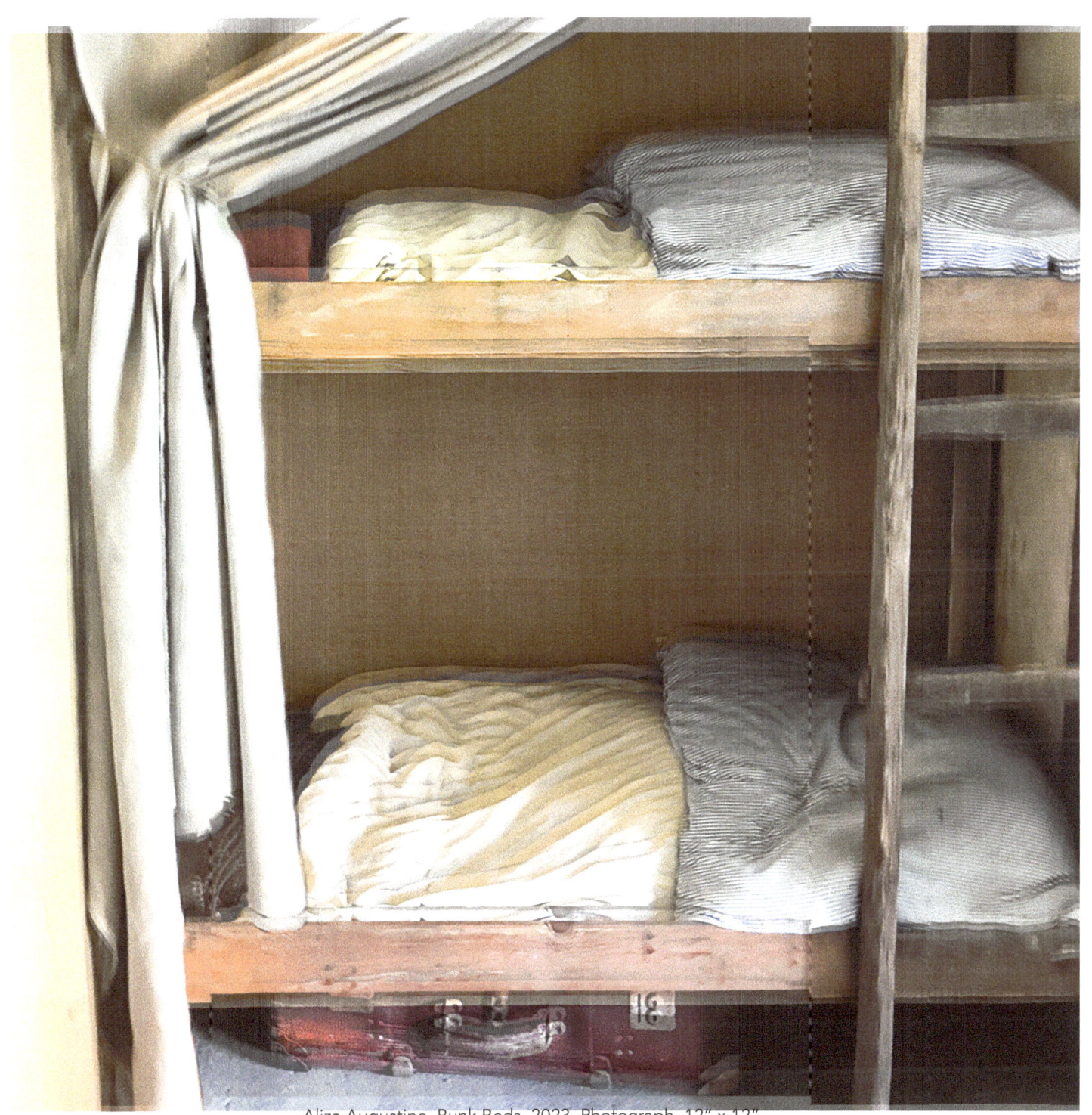

Aliza Augustine, Bunk Beds, 2023, Photograph, 12" x 12"

Documenting the Second Generation: Daughters of Holocaust Survivors
(below & opposite page)

This ongoing series is about the connection of the women in these portraits to their parents, Holocaust survivors. The series combines contemporary studio portraits with landscapes, which Aliza photographed in Europe, and personal photographs from their family collections to portray the story of the past and the present.

According to Aliza: "I conceived this project as a warning and a reminder while watching the Syrian refugees fleeing to Europe and being put into refugee camps. They brought to my heart and mind images of my family fleeing Vichy, France, in the dark of night for their lives in Dec., 1942.

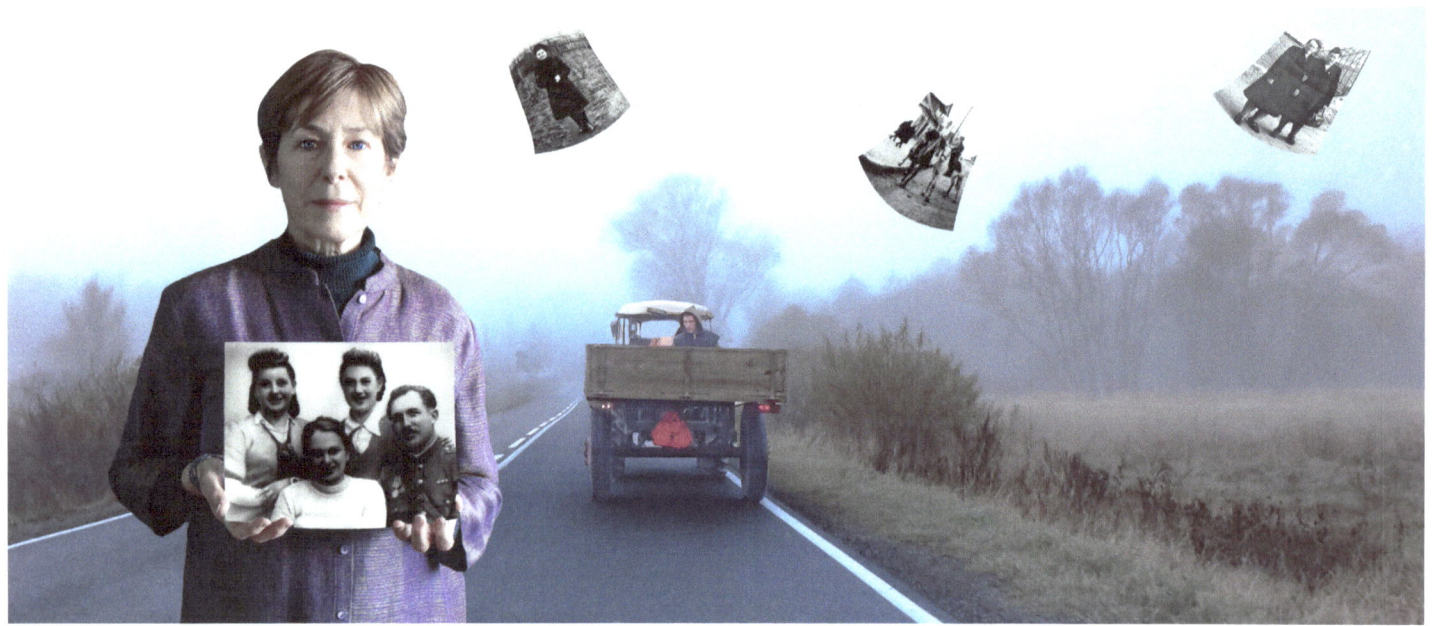

Aliza Augustine, Yona, 2023, Photograph, 42" x 18"

Perhaps this background makes me hypersensitive, living through the rise in fascism and the normalization of Trump did not help. My family and most of the children of survivors I know were deeply traumatized by this experience. Some of our parents are still alive. Soon we will be the only ones left who knew a survivor.

At the time I began this project, a few years ago, most of the United States had not yet realized what was to come– the huge rise in Holocaust denial, anti-Semitism, rampant police killings of Black men and women, and the rise of Naziism and White Nationalism.

Secretary of State Madeleine Albright, with her great understanding of history and prescience, said on April 6, 2018, in The New York Times "Fascism poses a more serious threat now than at any time since the end of World War II".

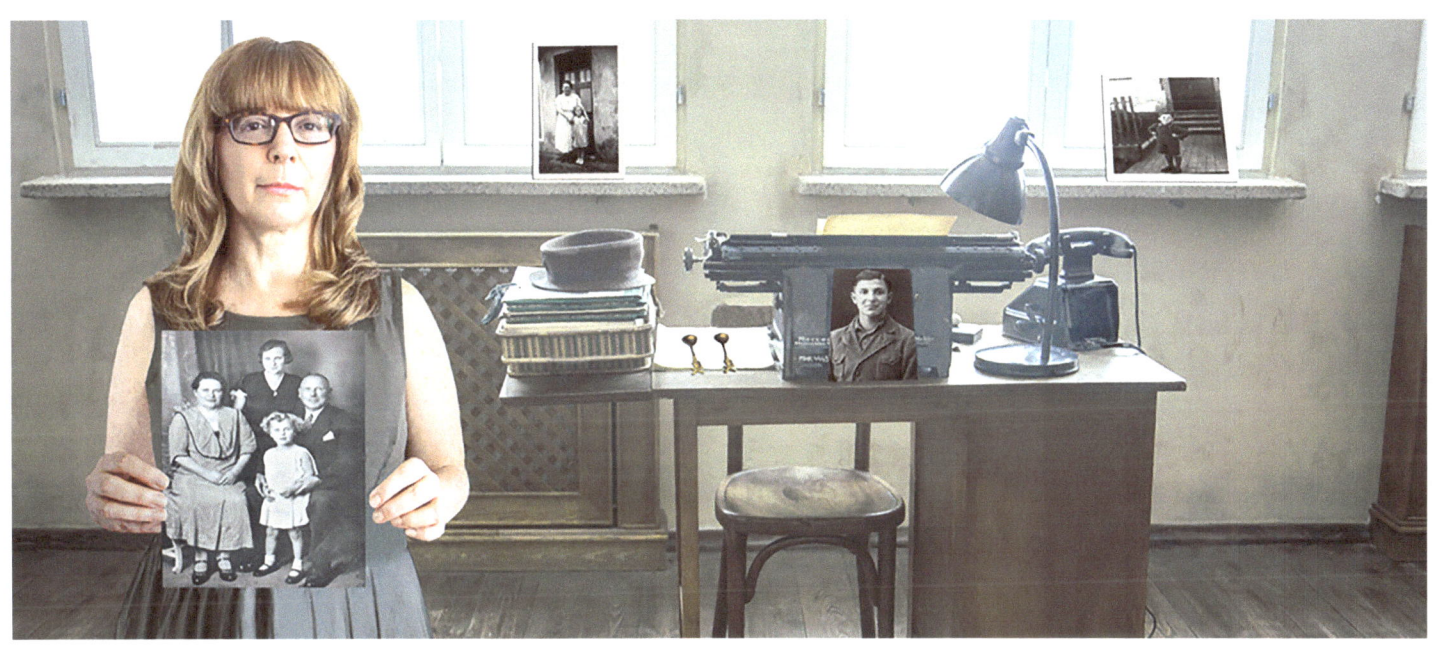

Aliza Augustine, Janet, 2017, Photograph, 42" x 18"

This ongoing series is about the conection of the women in these portraits to their parents, Holocaust survivors. We are living in a time reminiscent of pre-war Germany. This may sound inconceivable, but that is what most people in Germany and Europe said too.

The women in these photographs are contemporary, modern women here in America. To us, the Holocaust is not something old from a history book it is alive and visceral. I want you to see them in the same way.

This photographic series combines contemporary studio portraits with landscapes which I photographed in Europe and personal photographs from their family collections to portray the story of the past and the present."

FRANCIS CRISAFIO
Laurenceville, PA

Francis Crisafio was born and raised in the Laurenceville section of Pittsburgh, PA, and studied painting and printmaking at Carnegie Mellon University. A self-taught photographer, he has been included in group exhibitions at Photographic Resource Center, Boston; "The Fence", Brooklyn and Boston; Filter Festival/Space, Chicago; Center for Photography, Greenville, SC; A. Smith Gallery, Johnson City, TX; Los Angeles Center for Photography; The Center for Creative Photography, Tucson, AZ, PhotoNOLA, New Orleans; Aperture Foundation Gallery and Soho Photo Gallery, New York City; Philadelphia Photo Arts Center and The Print Center, Philadelphia, PA; Silver eye Center for Photography, Pittsburgh, PA; and the Providence Center for Photographic Arts, Providence, RI; amongst other venues.

Crisafio was a LensCulture Exposure Awards Finalist, 2015 at Photo London; a Semifinalist in The Print Center's 87th, 90th and 93rd ANNUAL International Competition, 2013, 2015 and 2018; a Fellow at the Silver Eye Center of Photography, Pittsburgh, 2017; and a Finalist twice for Exposure at Photographic Resource Center, Boston, 2018 and 2020.

Francis has been reviewed in Artscope Magazine, The Boston Globe, Feature Shoot, Hyperallergic, Lenscratch, A Photo Editor, Pittsburgh City Paper and Slate Magazine. His work is included in the permanent collection of Carnegie Mellon University and in private collections.

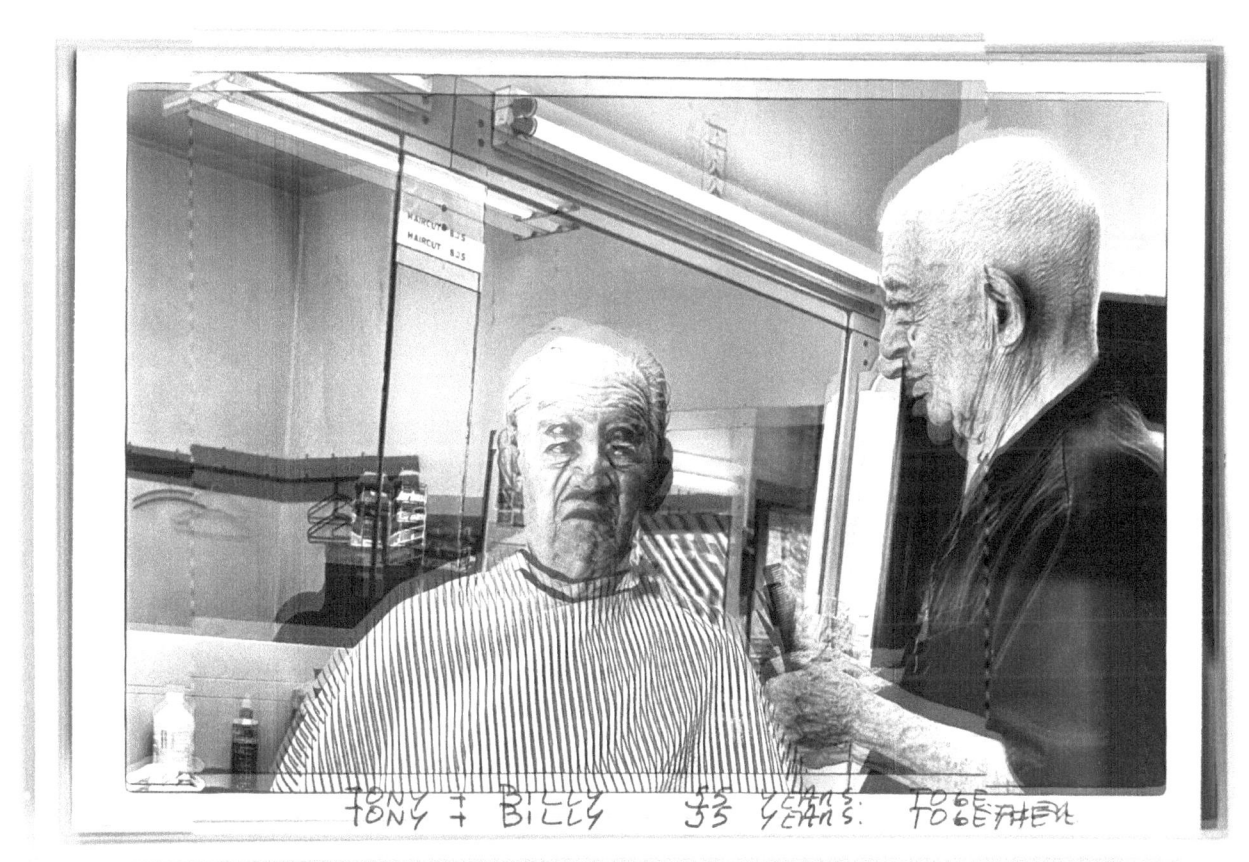

Francis Crisafio, Together series, 2004 - 2014, Photograph, 4" x 6"
Francis Crisafio, Together series, 2004 - 2014, Photograph, 4" x 6"

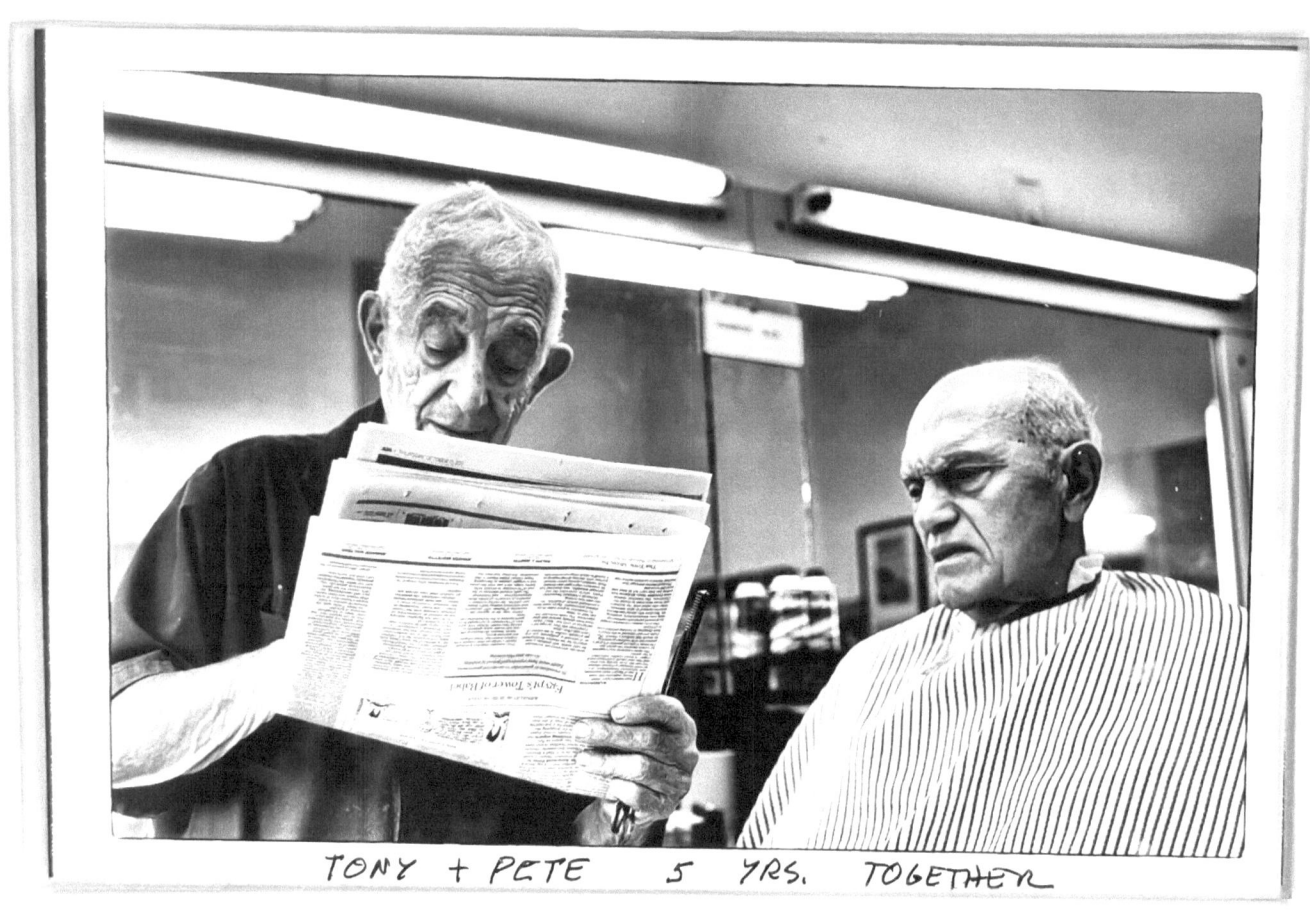

Francis Crisafio, Together series, 2004 - 2014, Photograph, 4" x 6"

Together Series
According to Francis: "I began photographing my father, Tony, and his customers, for the last 10 years of his life and career. The decade long documentation of this Italian, immigrant barber, who cut hair for eighty years before passing at the age of 95 in 2014, includes: still photographs, video, sound recordings and text. Tony's relationship with his customers was one of reciprocal devotion. His customers had a familial allegiance to him. Those customers included multi-generational families

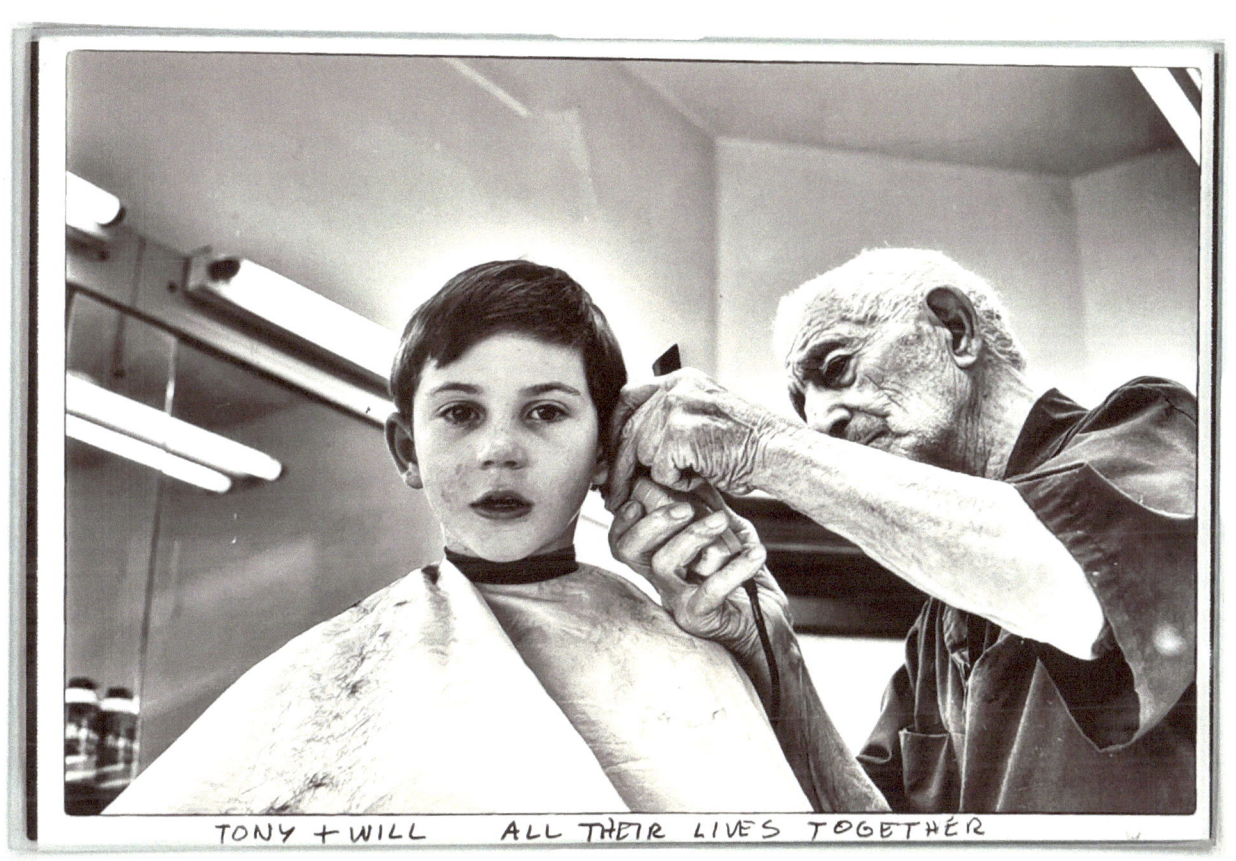

Francis Crisafio, Together series, 2004 - 2014, Photograph, 4" x 6"

as well as people who crossed demographic lines of age, class, gender and ethnicity. When the barbershop opened in 1929, and in the years following during the Great Depression, most customers were immigrants who came in for a haircut and a shave. The shop was located in a historic, working class neighborhood populated with steel mills and associated foundries called Lawrenceville, in Pittsburgh, PA. It still functions as a hair salon to this day.

MICHAEL PRIBICH
NY, NY

Michael Pribich is a visual artist living in New York City with artist Esperanza Cortes. He was born and raised in Northern California. Michael is interested in the artist's role in advancing ideas that lead to continual growth and change. His work uses labor to address themes of displacement and migration in both rural and urban settings. He explores the idea that labor can be viewed as cultural production, resulting in an expanded social space. Michael has participated in exhibitions and artist residencies throughout the USA, Mexico, Central Asia, and India. Recent exhibitions include *The Shape Of Things To Come* at Jadite Gallery, NYC; *Wheel Of Fortune* at Womb Space in Mexico City; and at the 360 Xochi Quetzal Residency in Chapala, Mexico. He completed a 2021 summer residency with the Nars Foundation in Brooklyn, and, in November 2021, he participated in a workshop in Sarajevo with Kuma International and Brodac Gallery dealing with memory, remembrance and contemporary forms of memorialization. Pribich has produced art projects with the Public Works Departments in Sacramento and Woodland, California. He has received a Pollock Krasner Award, and a Fulbright Award recommendation.

Seven Beauties (right)
My mother and her six sisters are the *Seven Beauties*. My grandparents crossed the border from México, became US citizens, and raised a family with nine children. The manila climbing rope represents a kind of border line through which immigrants cross. After reaching, pulling and dragging, they "climb" into a new society. Modified synthetic material bags speak to the resilience, determination and luck of immigrants to succeed in a new place who are climbing to create a new world. Heirloom buttons and brown shawls covering each bag show a kind of domestication of the raw material.

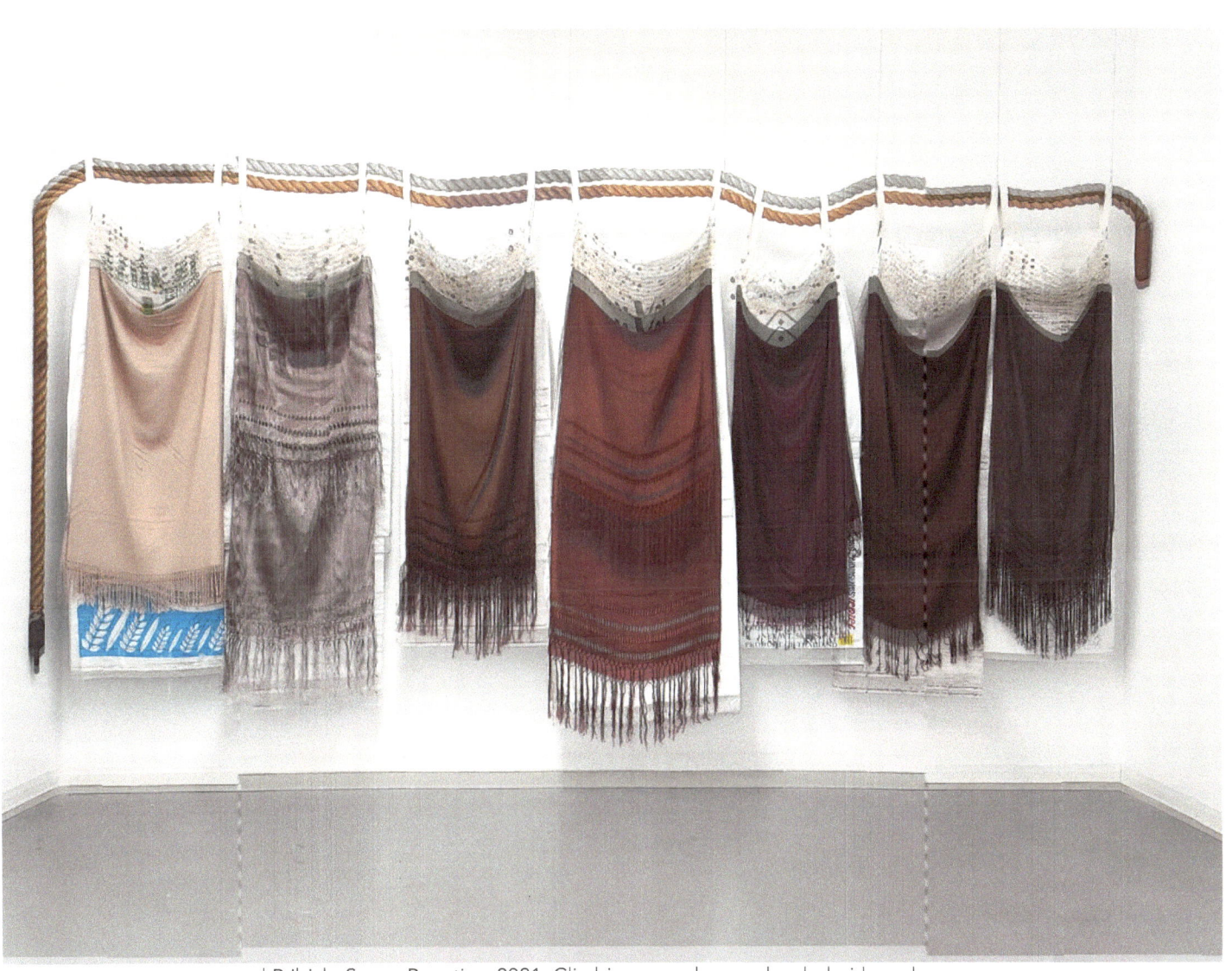

Michael Pribich, Seven Beauties, 2021, Climbing rope, brown shawls, heirloom buttons, ribbon, 83" x 160" x 4"

Black Support (right)
The concept of this work is informed by hybrid ideas of Méxican labor history, including the period when African slave labor was introduced into México. Beginning around 1521, port cities like Vera Cruz became terminus points for African slave ships. This interests me because of my own Méxican heritage, and because I want to participate in the revision of the historic amnesia that negates the outward existence of African slavery in México.

According to Michael: "The awful ache I feel when reminded of the dehumanized treatment of workers and human beings anywhere in the world pushes my art practice. Labor is the starting point, but my interest overlaps the treatment, and contributions of humans anywhere. My mother's parents immigrated from Chihuahua, México. My grandfather worked as a farm and cannery worker in and around Sacramento. My father's family immigrated from Croatia and worked as carpenters and service workers. At home while growing up, my father would always talk about work-related subjects. This family history shapes many of my ideas and informs my art. My mixed-race background gives me a hybrid position to explore the individual and collective circumstances of labor, so often determined by the intersections of race and class. My core belief is that recognizing labor as cultural production creates the conditions for an expanded social space."

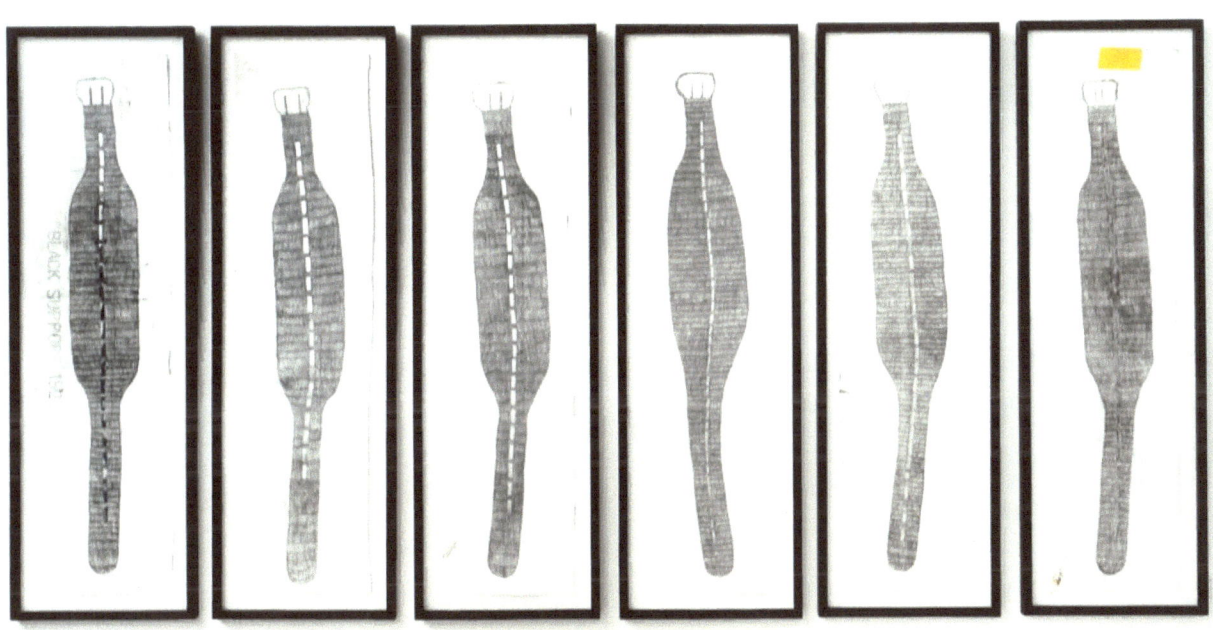

Michael Pribich, Black Support, 2021, Pencil on paper, 52" x 117" overall (6 frames 52" x 12" each)

NOELLE LORRAINE WILLIAMS
Newark, NJ

Noelle Lorraine Williams lives and works in Newark, NJ. She received her bachelors from the New School for Social Research and her masters from Rutgers University Newark. As a public humanities specialist, historian, artist, researcher and curator, her work examines the ways African Americans utilize culture to re-imagine liberation in the United States. She has exhibited and lectured in multiple venues including the Newark Museum, The African American Museum in Philadelphia, PA and the Jersey City Museum. Her work as an artist and curator has been reviewed in the New York Times, ArtNews, and other publications, including the Star-Ledger as a part of their profile on "The Newark School" and about her exhibition "Black Power! 19th Century Newark's First African American Rebellion". Her exhibition "Radical Women: Fighting for Power and the Vote in New Jersey!" was the recipient of the Giles R. Wright Award for contributions to African American History in NJ. She recently received the Creative Catalyst Grant from the City of Newark to produce two artistic interpretations of nineteenth century African American history.

Noelle is also a recipient of the 2021 Individual Artist Fellowship Award for Crafts from the New Jersey State Council on the Arts. She received a grant from the Audible's Newark Artist Collaboration for a five-billboard outdoor art installation in a highly trafficked, commuter area of Downtown Newark. Recently, she served as lead researcher on a project proposal for a Newark African American site as part of the National Park Service's National Underground Railroad Network to Freedom, one of Northern New Jersey's first federally funded sites. Along with Project for Empty Space, Noelle received the Abbey Mural Prize from the National Academy of Design for a mural on Black women suffragists.

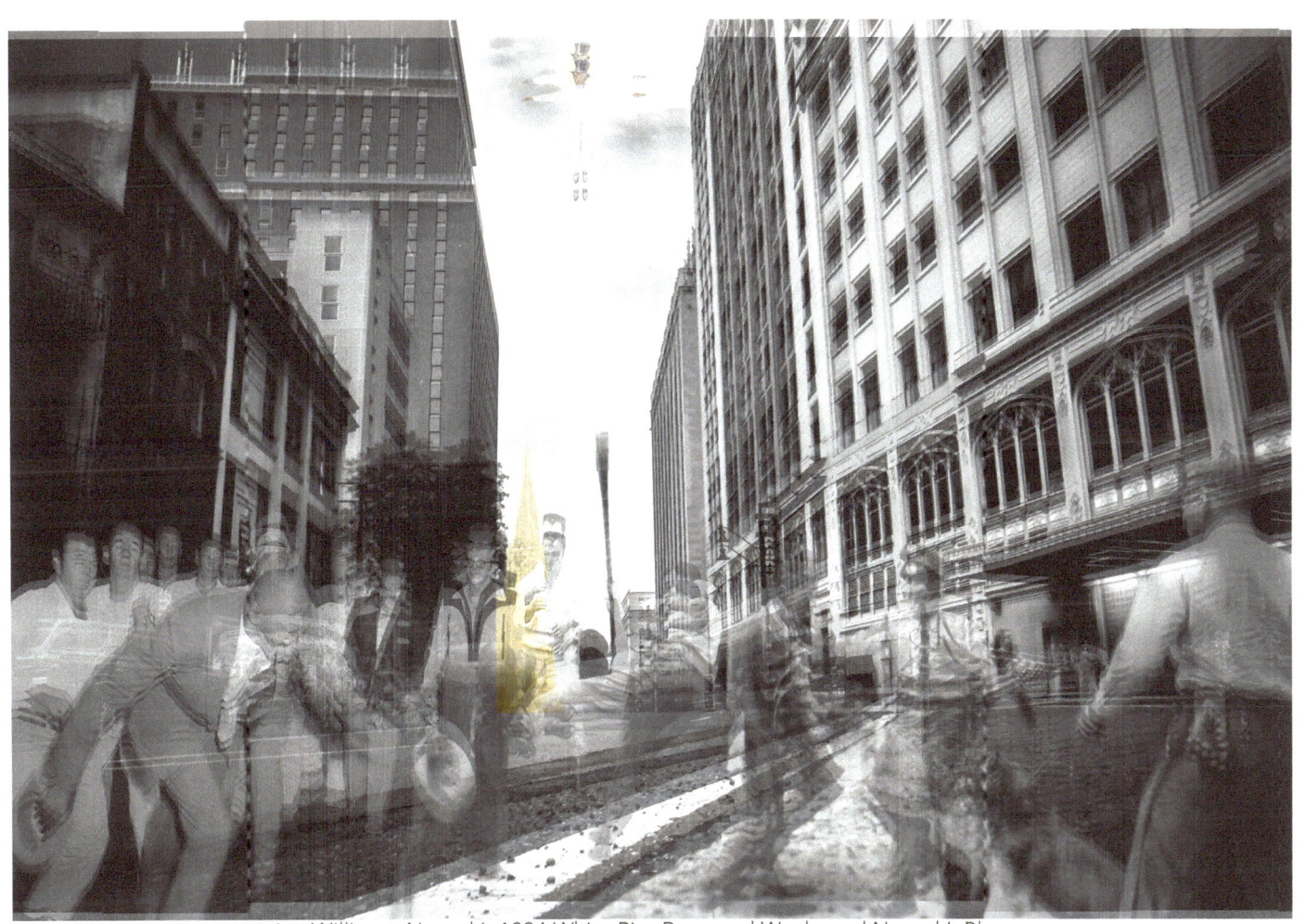

Noelle Lorraine Williams, Newark's 1834 White Riot Reverend Weeks and Newark's Black Activist, 2019, Aluminum Print, 12" x 18"

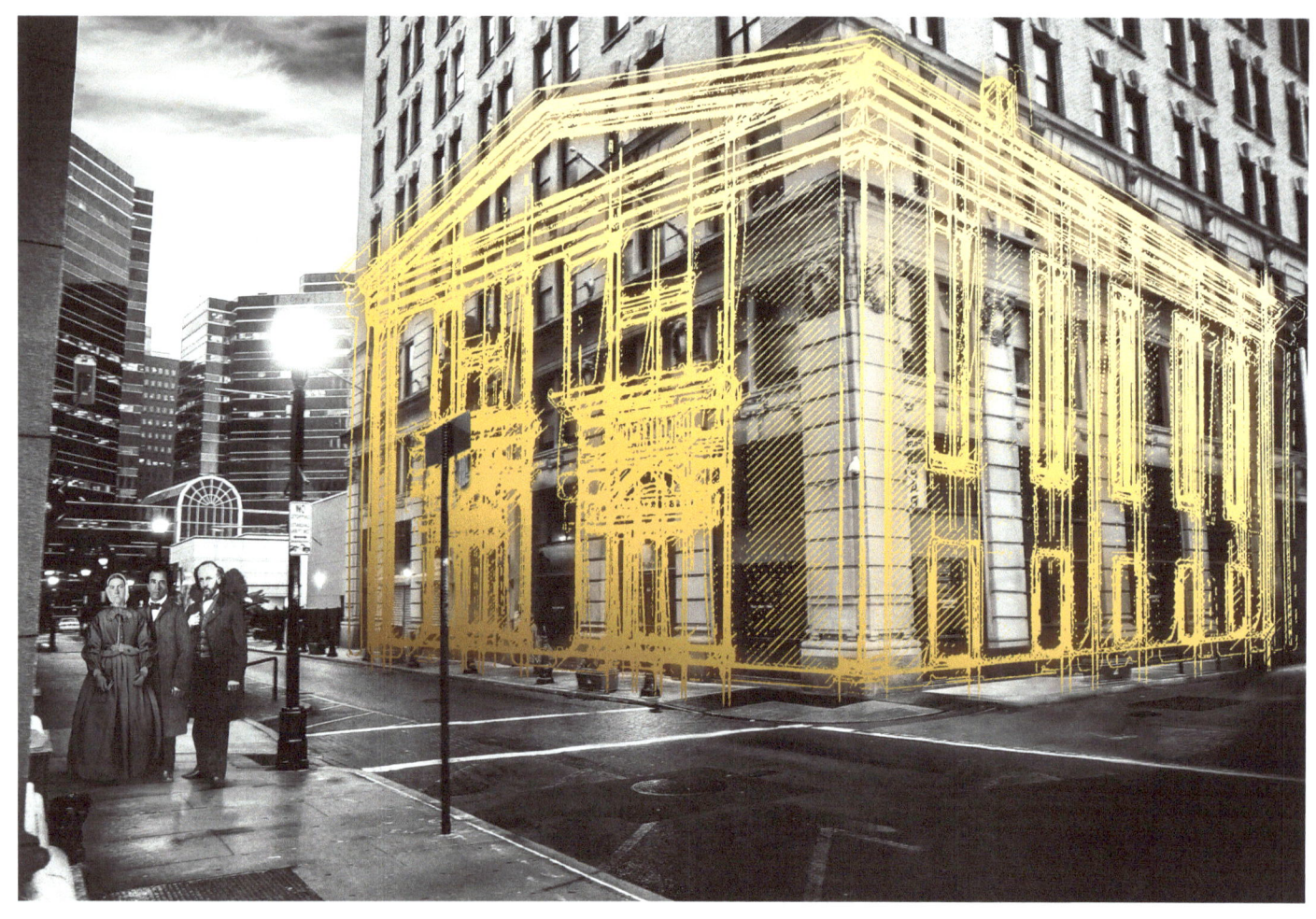

Noelle Lorraine Williams, Grimke, Weld and Beecher White Alliances and Newark's White Activist Nigger Church, 2018, Aluminum Print, 13" x 19"

Grimke, Weld and Beecher White Alliances and Newark's White Activist Nigger Church (above)
This work is from the *Monumental Spirit: Reimagined Sites of 19th Century Newark* series from the *Black Power! 19th Century* project. In Downtown Newark, the brother of Harriet Beecher Stowe, author of "Uncle Tom's Cabin" led a congregation that hosted anti-slavery speakers, including the famous abolitionist, Theodore Weld. Weld is pictured with his wife Angelina Grimke and Beecher. Though attended mainly by Whites, the church was called "nigger church" for its antislavery activism.

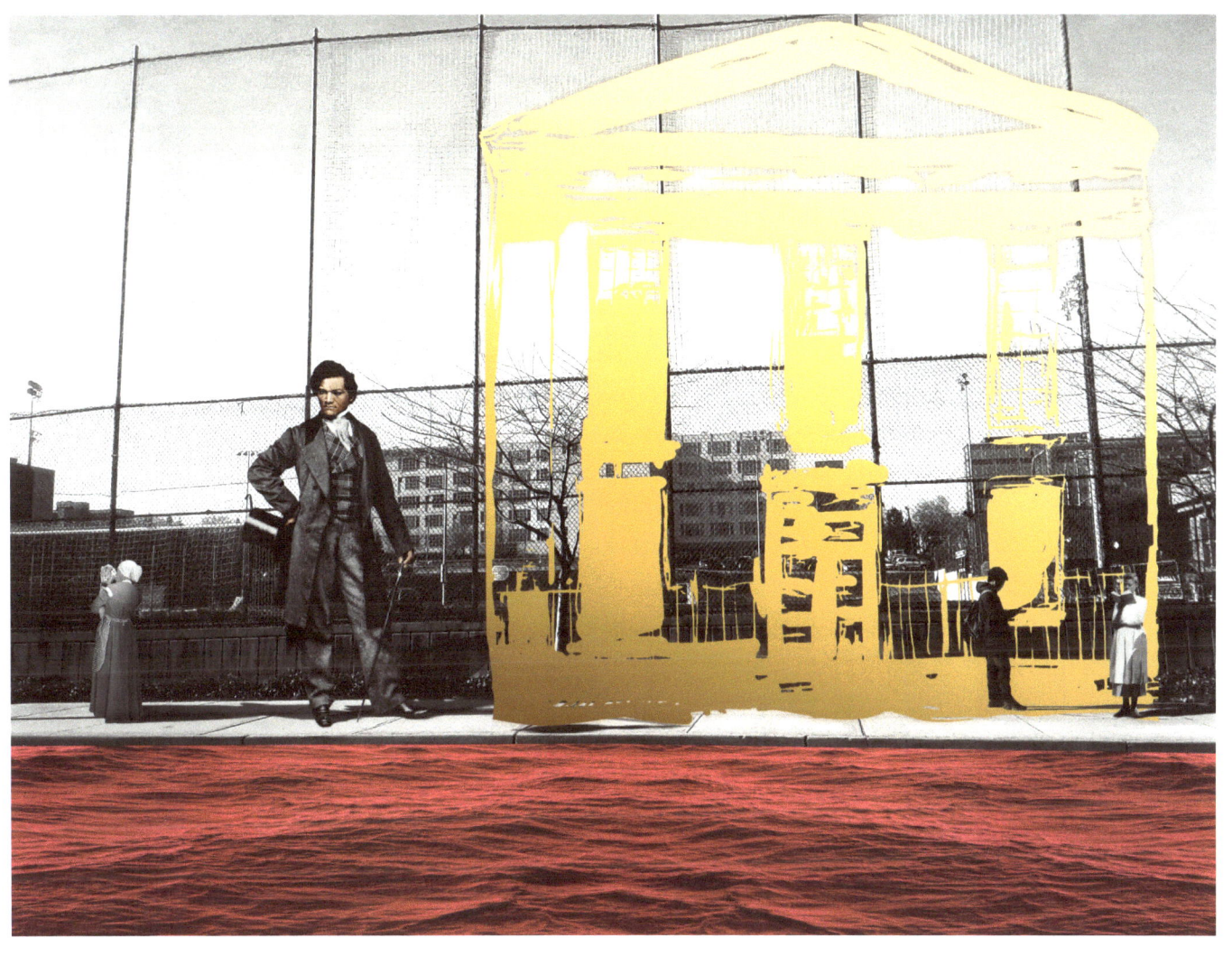

Noelle Lorraine Williams, Frederick Douglass Field and Plane Street Colored Church Freedom Seekers, 2021, Aluminum Print, 14" x 20"

WILLIE COLE
Newark, NJ

Willie Cole lives and works in New Jersey. Recently Cole's work was exhibited at the Museum of Arts and Design (New York, NY), Kemper Museum of Contemporary Art (Kansas City, MO), and Birmingham Museum of Art (Birmingham, AL). Selected public collections include Metropolitan Museum of Art, New York, NY; The Museum of Modern Art, New York, NY; Whitney Museum of American Art, New York, NY; Philadelphia Museum of Art, Philadelphia, PA; Virginia Museum of Fine Arts, Richmond, VA; Art Gallery of Ontario, Toronto, Canada; National Gallery of Art, Washington, D.C.

Willie's work has been the subject of several one-person museum exhibitions at the Museum of Modern Art, New York (1998), Bronx Museum of the Arts (2001), Miami Art Museum (2001), Tampa Museum of Art (2004), University of Wyoming Art Museum (2006), Montclair Art Museum (2006), College of Wooster Art Museum (2013-14).

In 2015, Willie's work was included in "Represent: 200 Years of African American Art" at the Philadelphia Museum of Art and "Wild Noise: Artwork from the Bronx Museum of the Arts" at El Museo Nacional de Bellas Artes, Havana. In 2016, his work was included in "Disguise: Masks and Global African Art" at the Brooklyn Museum. "Willie Cole: On-Site" opened at the David C. Driskell Center, University of Maryland and traveled to the Museum of Art at the University of New Hampshire, and Arthur Ross Gallery, Philadelphia in 2016. The following year, Cole had solo exhibitions at the Snite Museum of Art at the University of Notre Dame and at the College of Architecture and Design Gallery at the New Jersey Institute of Technology. In 2019, "Willie Cole: Beauties" opened at the Radcliffe Institute at Harvard University, as well as "Willie Cole: Bella Figura" at Alexander and Bonin, New York.

Collage 4 (opposite page)
Willie Cole's 'Collage 4,' made after he began his sculptures using hairdryers, is one of five collages constructed of pieces of cutout photocopies of black and white photographs he took of all sides of the same model hairdryer. The figurative shapes came from his recollection of a reproduction Mayan sculpture seen outside of a Cancun restaurant.

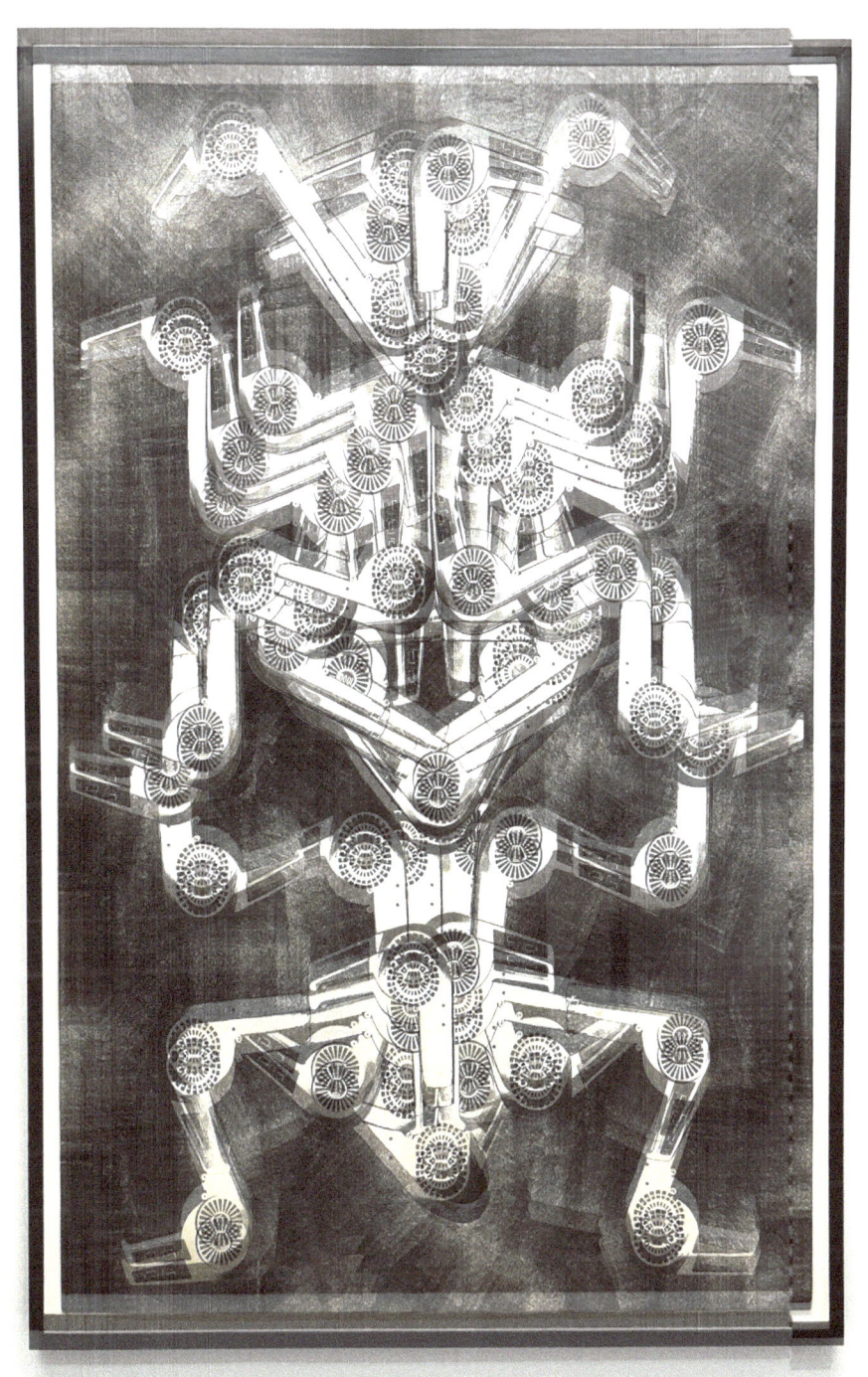

Willie Cole, Collage 4, 1990, Photocopy on paper, 60" x 40"
Willie Cole, Collage 4, 1990, Photocopy on paper, 60" x 40"

Domestic Shield (opposite page)
Willie Cole's iron scorched three-dimensional painting, *Domestic Shield XV*, recalls African body marking systems representative of distinct African ethnicities. Willie repurposes an ironing board into a configuration suggestive of a sterotypical African warrier's shield so every house could protect and empower its domestic workers or female member "slaves".

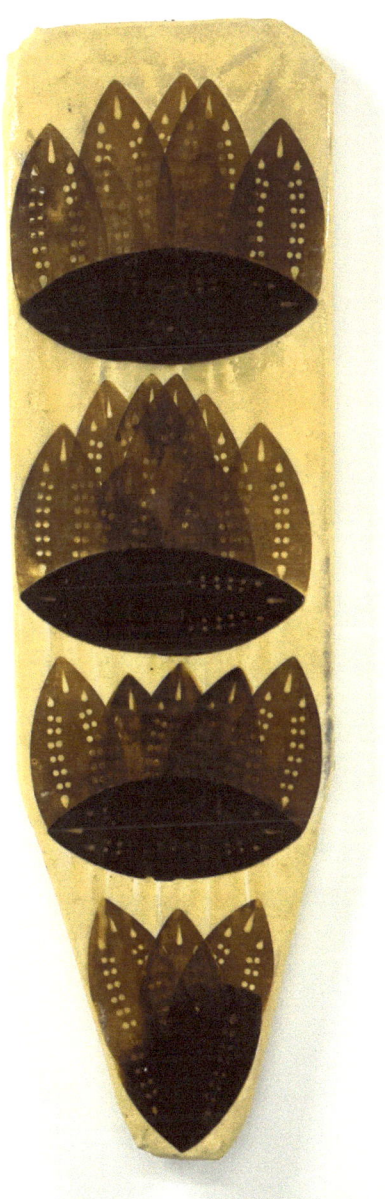

Willie Cole, Domestic Shield XV, 2020, Iron scorches on canvas with resin and wax, mounted on wood 54" x 16" x 2.5"

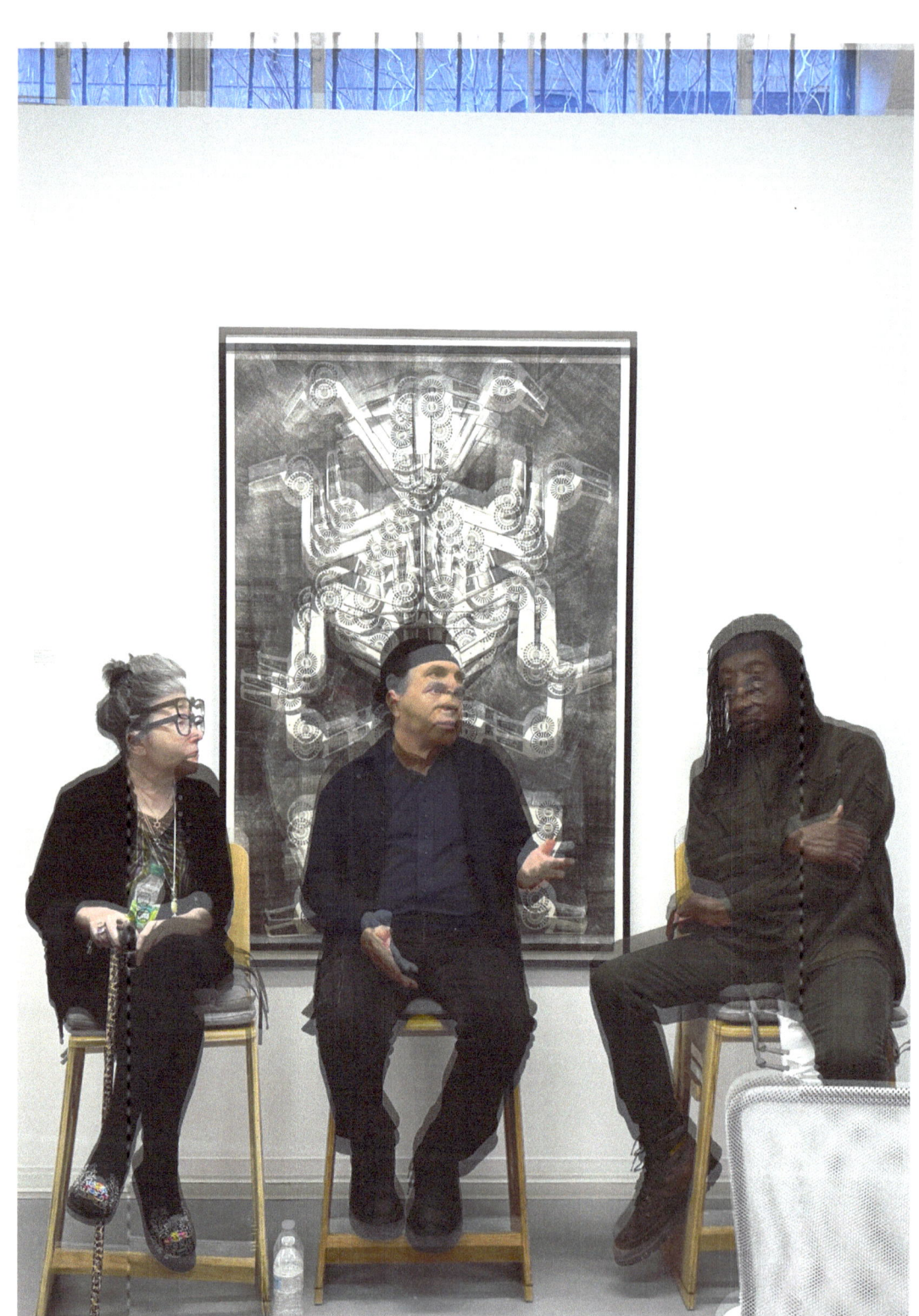

Artist Talks Weekend
Saturday 3/18/23 and
Sunday 3/19/23:

Left: Panel Discussion with artists, Aliza Augustine, Michael Pribich and Willie Cole speaking about their work.

Right: Adrienne Wheeler talks about her *White Dress Narrative*.

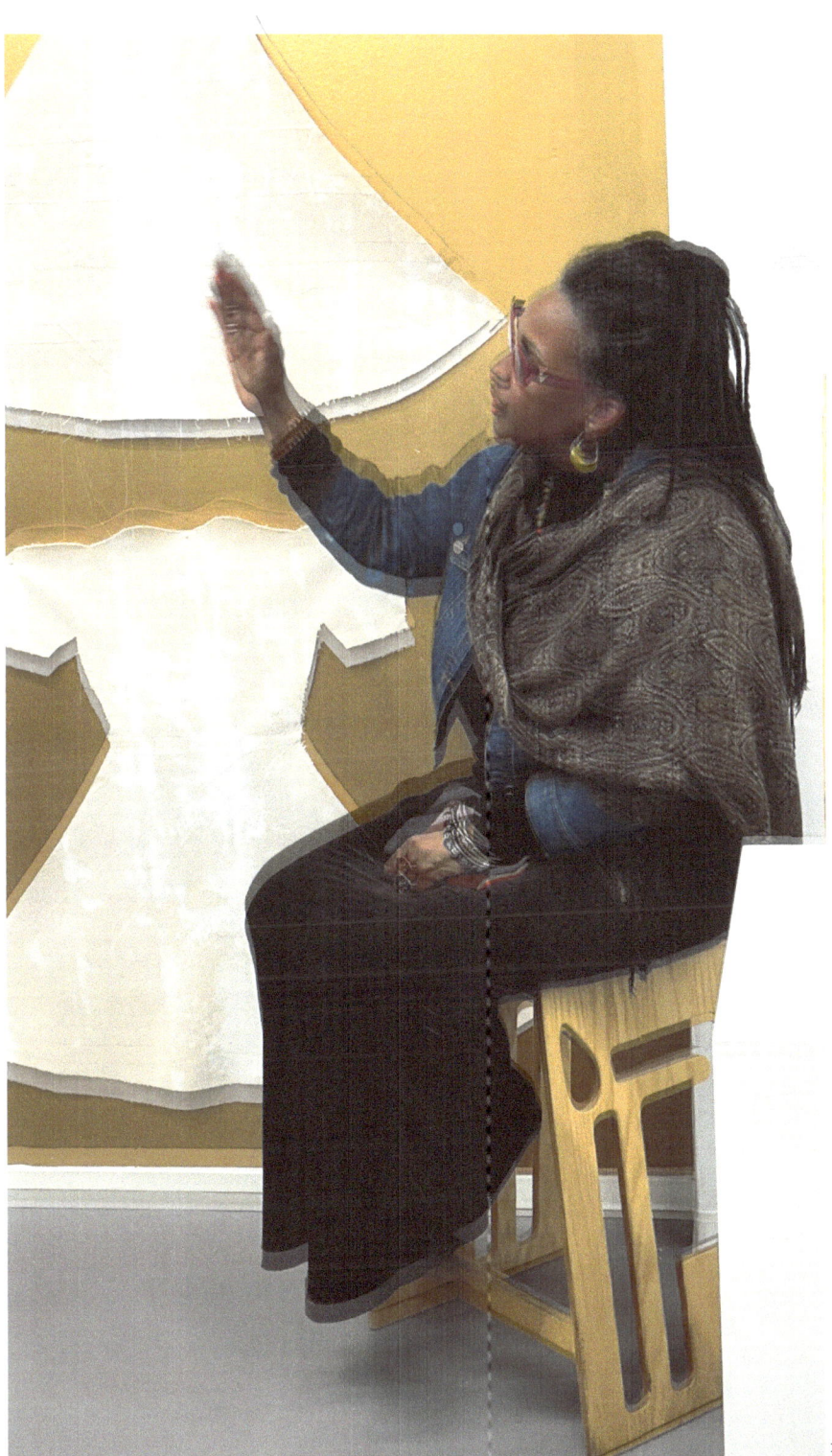

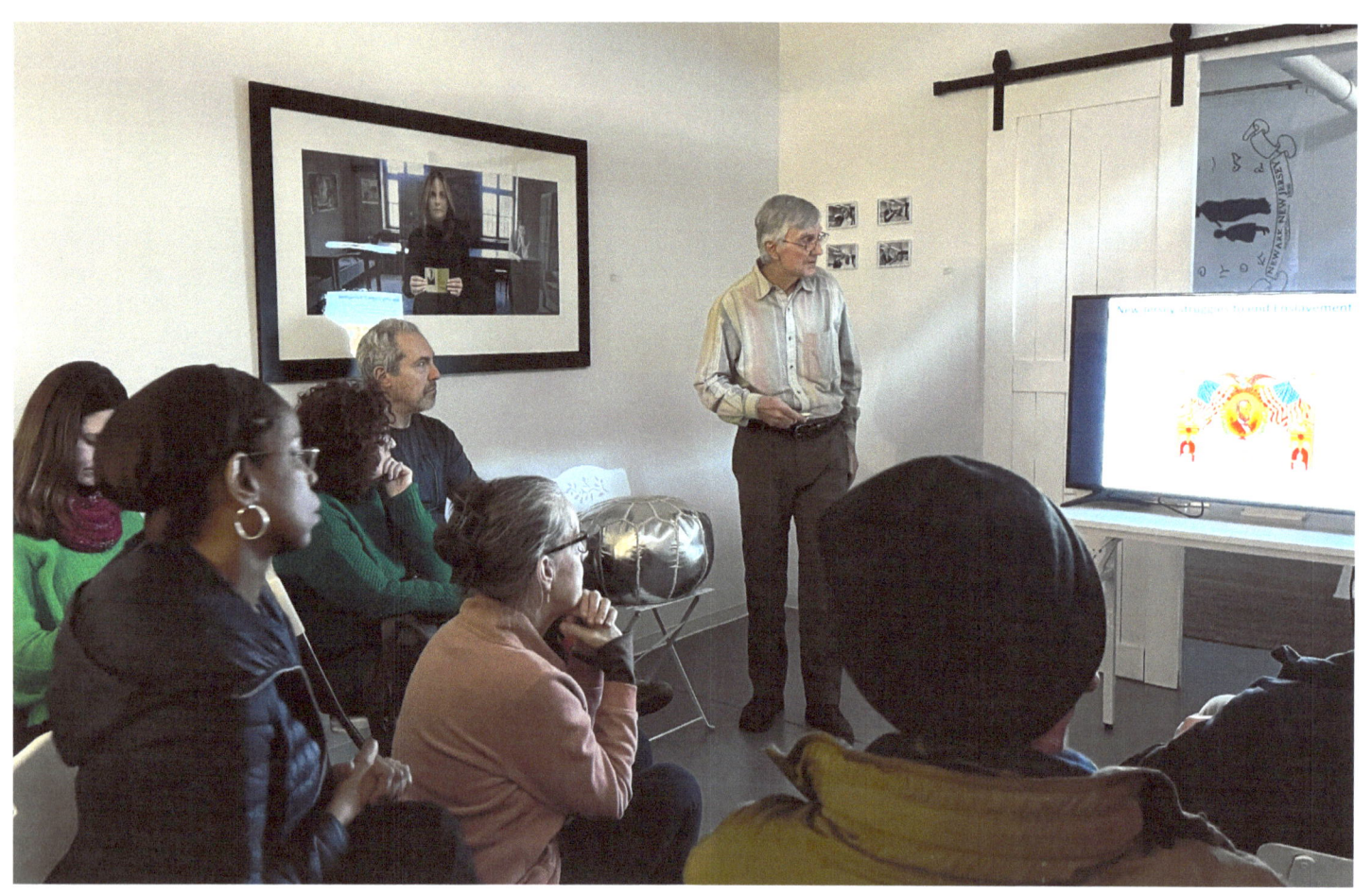

Artist Talks Weekend
NJ Historian and Author Rick Geffken speaks about his book, *Stories of Slavery in New Jersey,* and shows a powerpoint presentation.

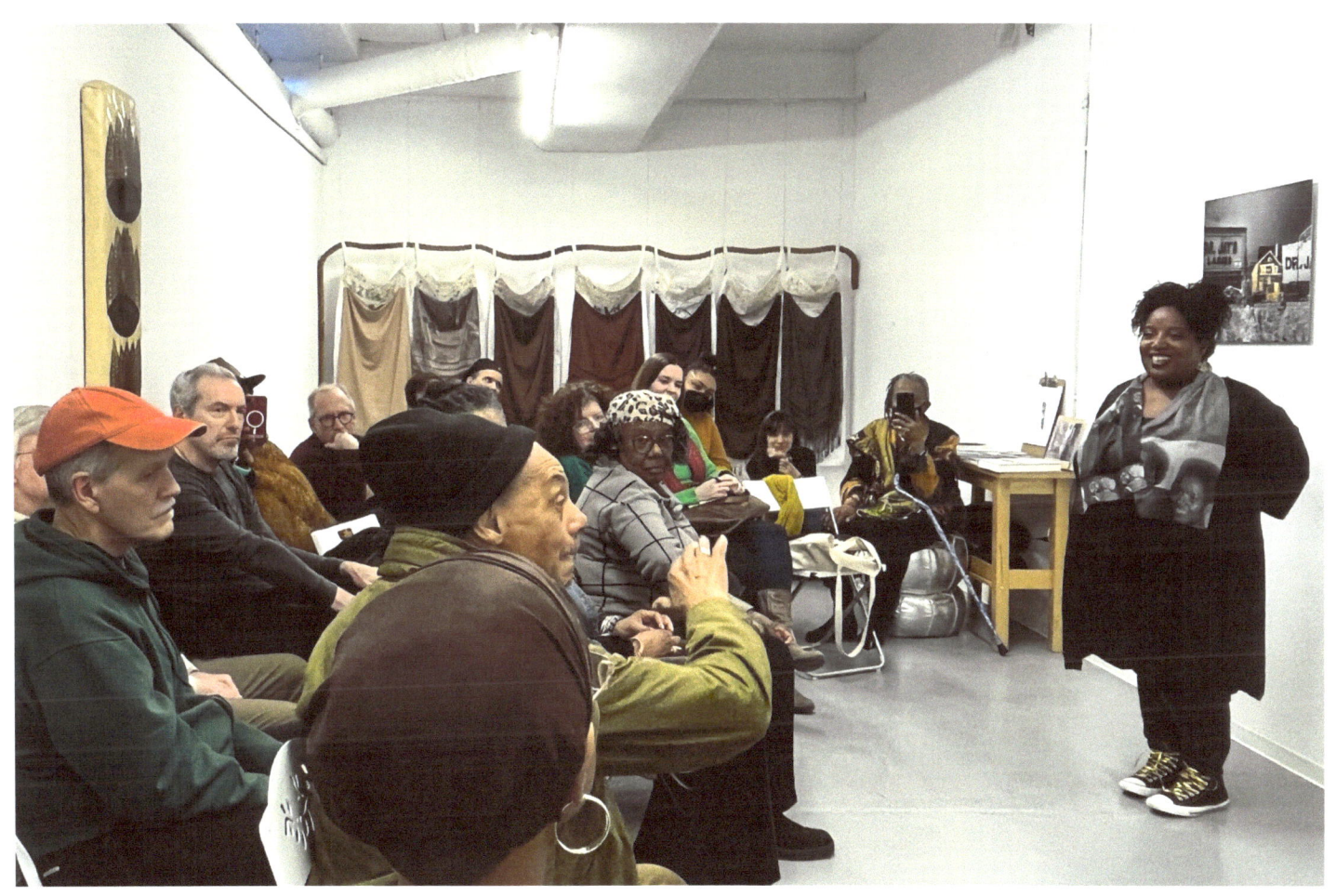

Noelle Lorraine Williams speaks about her work from the *Monumental Spirit: Reimagined Sites of 19th Century Newark*, part of her *Black Power! 19th Century* project.

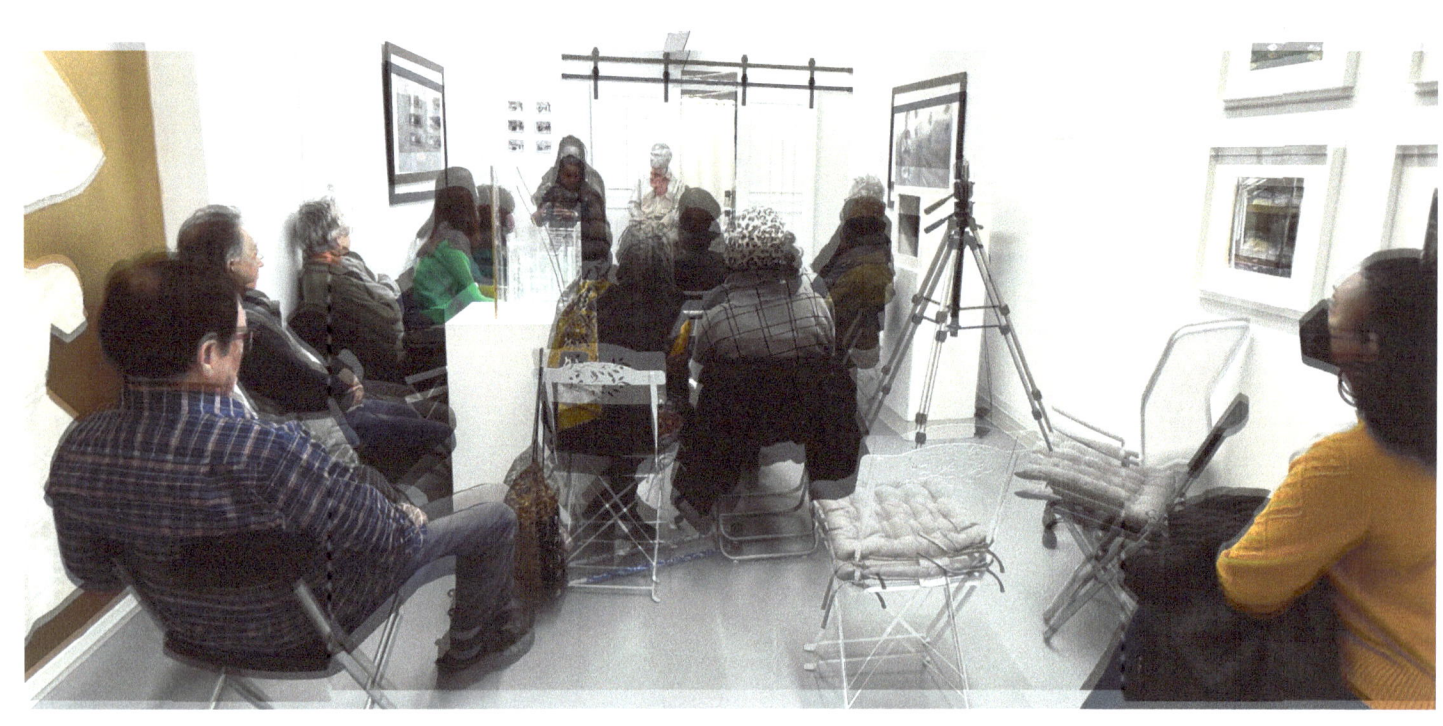

Panel Discussion with Adrienne Wheeler and Rick Geffken

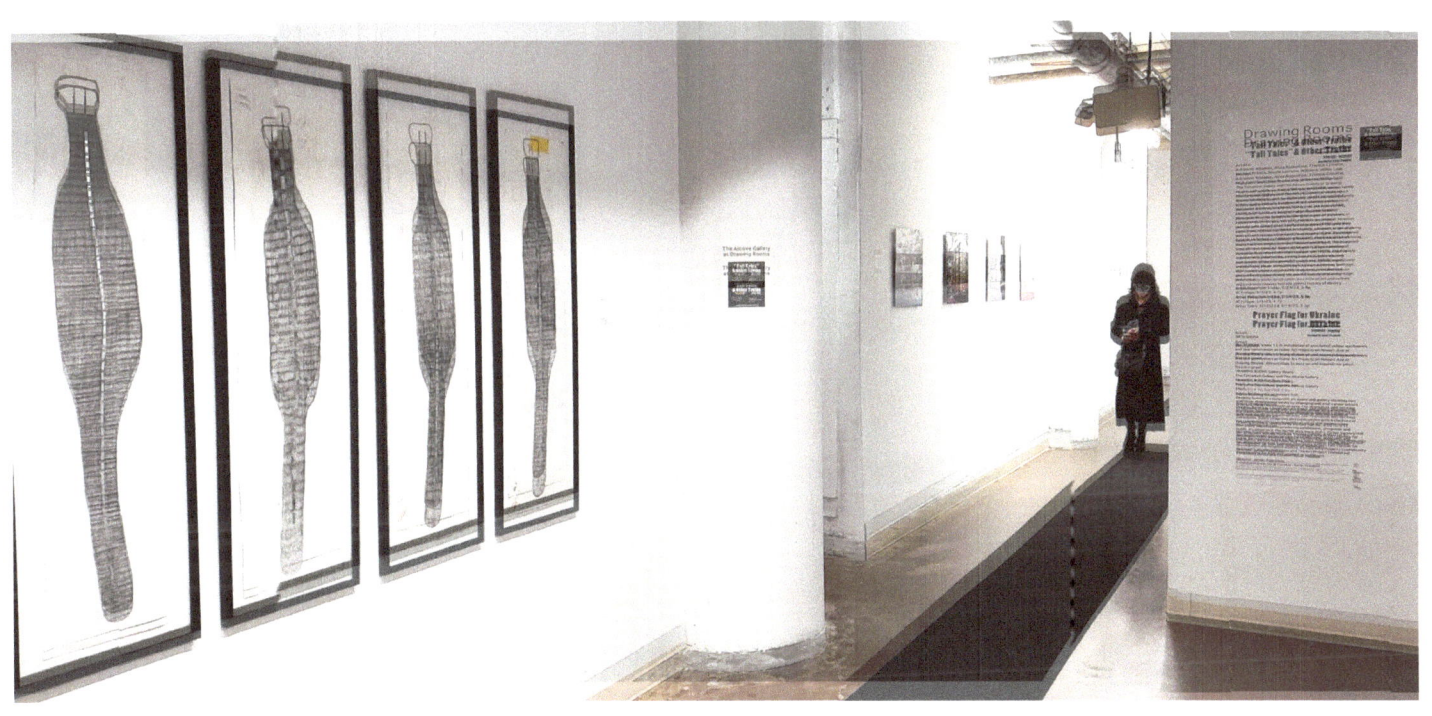
Curator Anne Trauben leaving the Alcove Gallery at Drawing Rooms

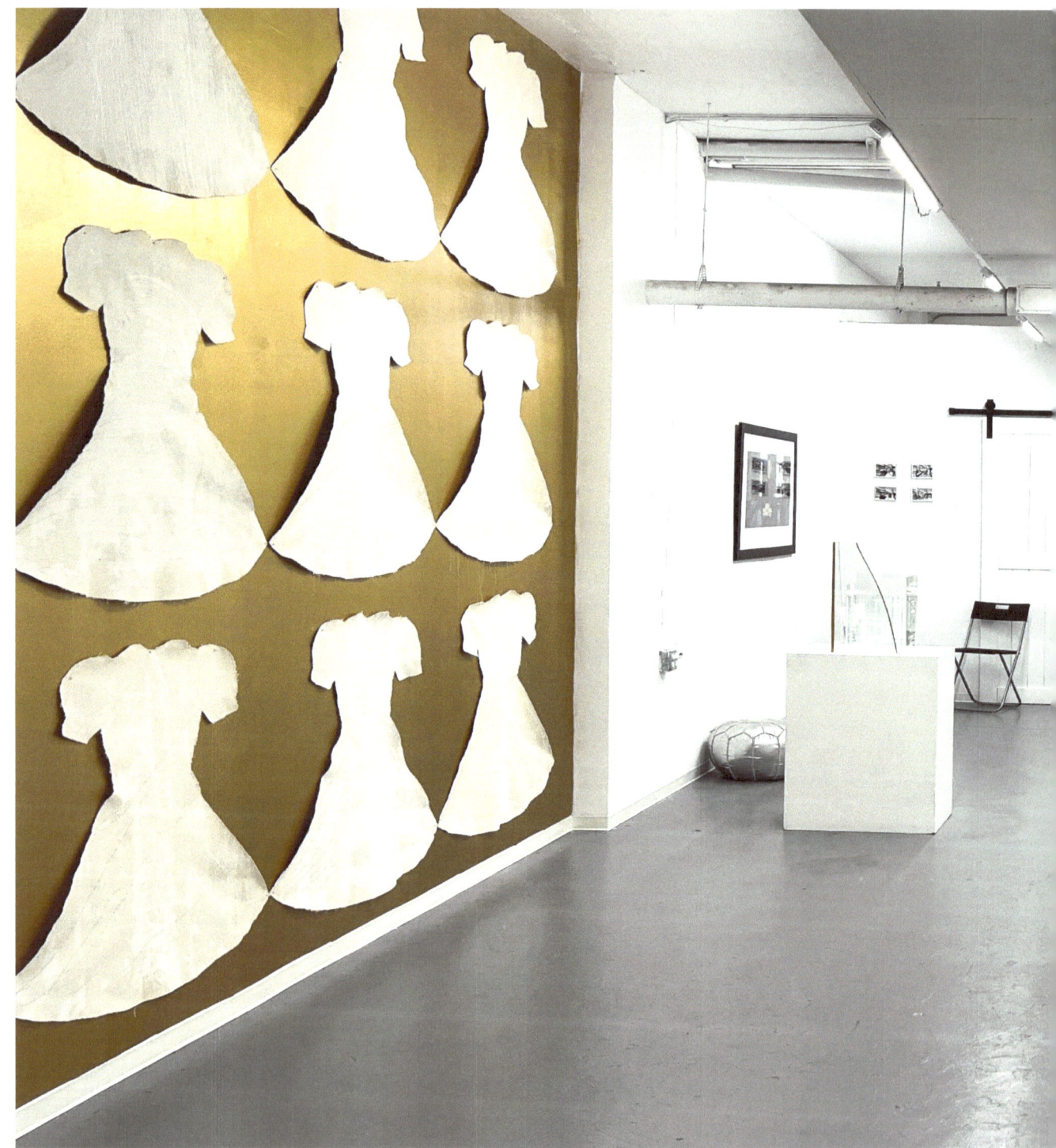

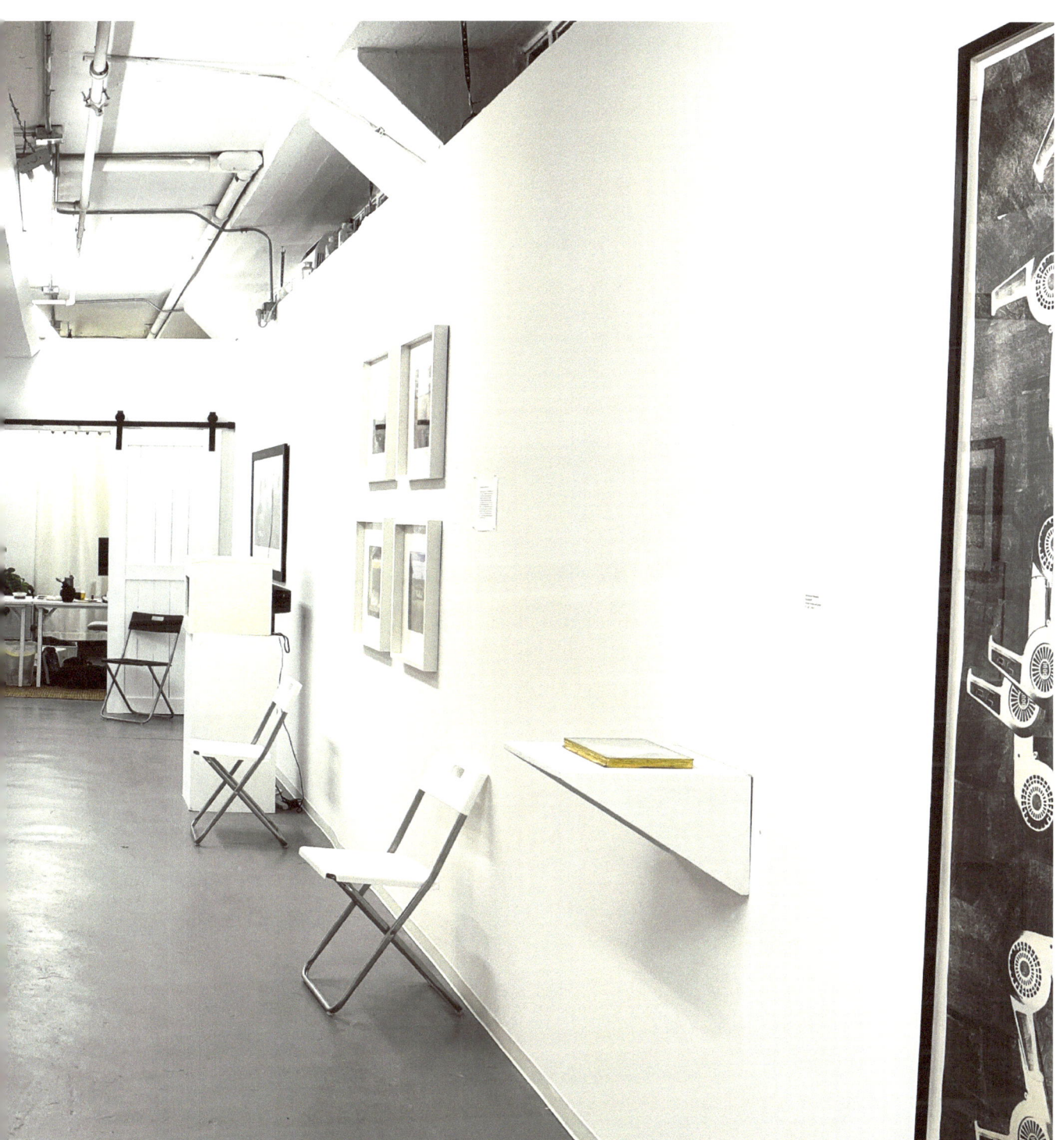

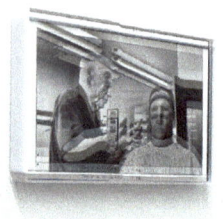 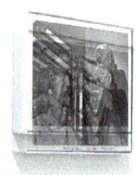 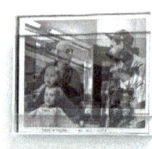 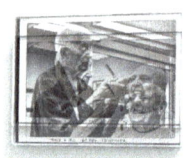 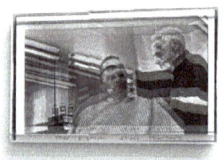

Installation View of Francis Crisafio's Together photographs

Victory Hall Press
926 Newark Ave
Jersey City, NJ 07306

ISBN: 9798391455064
April 2023

Editing and Design:
Anne Trauben
James Pustorino

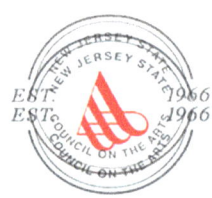 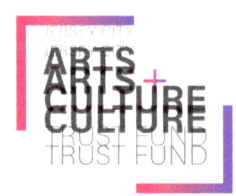 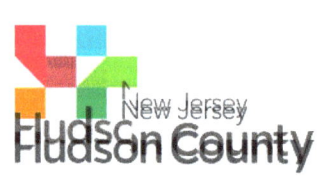

Made possible by funds from the New Jersey State Council on the Arts, a partner agency of the National Endowment for the Arts.

Supported by public funds from the Jersey City Arts and Culture Trust Fund.

This program is made possible in part by funds from the New Jersey State Council on the Arts /Department of State, a partner agency of the National Endowment for the Arts, administered by the Hudson County Office of Cultural and Heritage Affairs, Thomas A. DeGise, County Executive, and the Board of Chosen Freeholders.

www.ingramcontent.com/pod-product-compliance
Lightning Source LLC
Chambersburg PA
CBHW051934210526
45473CB00006B/2239